Classic Knits

Copyright 2014 © Knit Picks

All rights reserved. This book or any portion thereof may not be reproduced or used in any manner whatsoever without the express written permission of the publisher except for the use of brief quotations in a book review.

Printed in the United States of America

First Printing, 2014

ISBN 978-1-62767-041-8

Versa Press, Inc
800-447-7829

www.versapress.com

CONTENTS

Heirloom Layette Set — 4

Kitty Hat, Booties & Mitts Set — 14

Little Old Man Jacket — 20

Peter & Wendy — 24

Sleepy Kitty Stuffed Toy — 30

Striped Pullover — 36

HEIRLOOM LAYETTE SET

by Kerin Dimeler-Laurence

FINISHED MEASUREMENTS
Blanket: 36x33"
Bonnet: 0 (3, 6) mos.
Sweater: 0 (3, 6) mos.

YARN
Knit Picks Stroll Sock (75% Superwash Merino Wool, 25% Nylon; 462 yards/100g): Bare 23852, 4 hanks.

NEEDLES
US 4 (3.5 mm) 16" or longer circular needles plus straights for border, or size to obtain gauge
US 3 (3.25 mm) straight needles, plus circular or DPNs for small circumferences; spare DPNs for I-cord

NOTIONS
Yarn Needle
Stitch Markers
Scrap yarn or Stitch Holder
7 (8, 8) .5" buttons for sweater

GAUGE
Blanket: 20 sts and 34 rows = 4" in garter lace pattern on larger needles, blocked.
Bonnet and Sweater: 25 sts and 50 rows (25 ridges) = 4" in Garter st on smaller needles, blocked.

Heirloom Layette Set

Notes:
Beautiful Orenburg-style lace adorns this layette set, sure to become a treasured keepsake.

W&T (Wrap and Turn):
Work until the stitch to be wrapped. Bring yarn to the front of the work, slip next st as if to purl, return the yarn to the back; turn work and slip wrapped st onto RH needle. Continue across row.

Picking up wraps: Work to the wrapped st. Insert the RH needle under the wrap(s), then through the wrapped st Kwise. Knit the wrap(s) together with the wrapped st.

DIRECTIONS
Blanket
The blanket is made in one piece, with a border knit on.

Center Panel
Using larger circular needles, CO 170 sts. Work in Garter St (Knit every row) for 5". On the next row, K 25, PM, work across all 120 sts of Blanket chart, PM, K remaining 25 sts to end. Continue working back and forth, working 25 sts on each edge in Garter st, and working from the Blanket chart between markers. Work through row 90 of the chart, then work rows 31-90 once more; continue to row 120 of the chart. Work in Garter st for 5"; BO all sts loosely.

Edging
Start the edging in the center of one side; this will make the join less obvious.

With larger straight needles, loosely CO 4 sts. Begin working from Blanket Edging chart. On each RS row, work the last P2tog st by slipping the last st Pwise, picking up a st from the edge of the blanket, and purling those two sts together, joining the edging. PU one blanket st in each Garter ridge on the sides, and PU one stitch for each two stitches across the top and bottom.

To work corners: When you are two stitches or two rows (one garter ridge) from a corner, work four rows of the chart into each stitch or row by purling the edge stitches of two consecutive RS rows into the same stitch or row of the blanket. Work four rows into the corner in the same manner, and then repeat with the next two rows or stitches of the adjacent side; 20 rows of the Border will be worked into 5 picked up stitches at each corner. This creates ease around the corner, to prevent the border from binding.

When you have worked all the way around the blanket, you should be on Row 8 of the chart. Start checking this after the last corner, you can pick up an extra row/ridge stitch once or twice without it being noticeable if it's spread out. BO the first four sts as shown on Row 8, then break yarn, leaving a generous 12" tail. With the yarn tail, graft the remaining live sts to the cast on row at the beginning of the edging.

Finishing
Weave in ends, wash and block.

Bonnet
A sweet Garter st bonnet is trimmed with a simple lace border and an I-cord tie.

With smaller needles, loosely CO 63 (69, 75) sts. Work in Garter st (knit every row) for 6 rows.

On the next (RS) row, begin working from Bonnet Border chart on row 1, working sts 1-7, then repeating sts 8-13 8 (9, 10) times; continue chart to the end of the row.

After finishing the first 14 rows, work rows 15-26 3 (4, 5) times thus; work to st 8 of the chart, PM, then work in Garter st to the last 8 sts of the row, PM, and continue with sts 14-21 of the chart. This will create a lace border along the sides.

On the next (RS) row, knit to the last 8 sts, remove marker; put these sts on a stitch holder or scrap yarn. Turn. Repeat on the next row: 16 sts (8 on each edge) on holders, 47 (53, 59) sts on needles.

Crown
Round 1, sizes 0 (6) mos: Knit, placing markers after every 12 (15) sts.
Round 1, size 3 mos. only: K2tog, K12, PM, (K13, PM) twice, K to last 2 sts, SSK.
All sizes: CO 1 st after last st worked; PM and join to work in the round. 48 (52, 60) sts.
Round 2: Purl.
Round 3: *(K to 2 sts before marker, K2tog, SM)*; repeat between *s around. 4 sts removed.
Repeat rounds 2-3 6 (7, 9) more times: 20 sts remain.
Round 4: *(P to 2 sts before marker, P2tog, SM)*; repeat between *s around. 16 sts.
Round 5: *(K to 2 sts before marker, K2tog, SM)*; repeat between *s around. 12 sts.
Round 6: (P1, P2tog, SM) four times. 8 sts remain.
Round 7: K2tog 4 times, removing markers. 4 sts.

Break yarn. With a yarn needle, pass the yarn tail through the remaining live sts, and pull tight to close the hole. Pass the tail to the inside of the work.

I-Cord Ties
Simple I-cord ties are added to the front of the bonnet. You could also use satin ribbon for the same purpose.

With a DPN in smaller needle size, PU and K 4 sts along either corner of the bonnet (2 sts stitch-wise, 2 sts row-wise). *Slide the sts to the other end of the needle. Pull the yarn firmly behind all sts, and knit across the row, creating a tube.* Repeat between *s for 8 (9, 10)". Break yarn. Use yarn needle to pass the tail through the live sts; pull tight to close end of cord. Bury the end in the cord.

Make another I-cord tie at the other front corner in the same way.

Finishing

Place each set of 8 held sts under the crown onto spare needles. From the WS, attach yarn and work a 3-needle BO over these sts, working from the edge inward. Break yarn and use the yarn tail to close any gaps between the lace border and the crown. Weave in ends, wash and block.

Sweater

This little raglan sweater has the same simple lace as the bonnet and buttons up the front. The sleeves are worked flat up to the underarms and seamed; they are joined to the body and worked to the neck in one piece.

Sleeves (make 2)

With smaller needles, CO 34 (36, 38) sts. Work in Garter st for 6 rows. On the next (RS) row, begin working from Sleeve Cuff chart, following the line for your size, and repeating sts 9-14 four times, then working across row to last st indicated for your size. After all 14 rows have been worked, 38 (40, 42) sts are on the needles.

Increase Row: KFB, K to last st, KFB. 2 sts added.

The sweater will be worked in Garter st from this point. Work an Increase Row on the next row, then every other row 8 (9, 10) times. 56 (60, 64) sts on the needles. Work in Garter st for 2 (3, 5) rows. Break yarn and place sleeve on a stitch holder or scrap yarn.

Make second sleeve the same way.

Body

The body begins at the hem and has a diamond border running along the hem and up the front. Buttonholes are worked on both sides of the front; sew buttons over the holes in the side you wish to be the button band. The buttonholes are included in the Sweater Border chart at sts 4 and 5, and 27 and 28, on rows 7 and 19. Body decreases are worked at the same time as the chart is worked, read through entire section before proceeding.

With smaller needles, CO 145 (151, 157) sts. Work in Garter st for 6 rows. On the next row, begin working from Sweater Border chart, repeating sts 13-18 20 (21, 22) times. Work through the first 14 rounds. On the next row, work from chart to stitch 13, K 25 (27, 28), PM to mark underarm, K 69 (71, 75), PM to mark underarm, K to last 13 sts, work sts 19-31 from chart. Continue working as established, working from chart at edges and in Garter st between, for 49 (53, 57) rows (four repeats of rows 15-26 of the chart, plus 1 (5, 9) rows).

At the same time, decrease the body:
Row 40 of the body (8th row of second repeat): Work in pattern to first marker, SM, K2tog, work in pattern to end.

Row 60 of the body (4th row of fourth repeat): Work in pattern to 2 sts before first marker, SSK, SM, K to next marker, SM, K2tog, work in pattern to end.

3 sts decreased; 142 (148, 154) sts on the needles, 68 (70, 74) for the back, 37 (39, 40) each front.

Yoke

The sleeves are joined to the body and the yoke is decreased to the neckline, which is shaped with short rows. Work Raglan shaping and Neckline instructions at the same time, read through both sections before proceeding. The neckband is knit directly on to the body, making this a self-finishing garment.

On the next row, join sleeves to body.

Work in pattern to 3 sts before first marker. *Place the next 6 sts on holder or scrap yarn, removing marker. Place one sleeve back on the needles, Slip the first 4 and last 4 sts onto scrap yarn. On body, PM and K across center sts of sleeve; PM and join to next live st of body*. Knit to 3 sts before next marker, repeat between *s. Work in pattern to the end of the row; 226 (240, 254) total sts on the needles, 34 (36, 37) each front, 48 (52, 56) each sleeve, 62 (64, 68) across the back.

Body Decrease Row: Work in pattern to 2 sts before first marker, *K2tog, SM, knit across sleeve, SM, SSK*, K to 2 sts before next marker, repeat between *s, work in pattern to end. 4 sts decreased on the body.

Raglan Decrease Row: *Work in pattern to 2 sts before marker, K2tog, SM, SSK*, repeat between *s three more times, work in pattern to end. 8 sts decreased.

Work a Body Decrease Row on the next 4 (3, 3) rows. Work a Raglan Decrease row on the next row, then every other row 15 (17, 19) times. 16 sts remain across each sleeve and 22 sts across the back neck.

Neckline

On row 16 (20, 24) of the raglan decreases, begin neckline shaping:
Row 1: Work in pattern to the last 6 sts, W&T.
Row 2: Repeat row 1.
Row 3: Work in pattern to 7 sts before wrapped sts, K4, W&T.
Row 4: Repeat row 3. From this point, work sts that had been in charted lace in Garter st.
Row 5: Work in pattern to 2 sts before wrapped st, W&T.
Row 6: Repeat row 5.
Row 7: Work in pattern to 1 st before wrapped st, W&T.
Rows 8-10: Repeat row 7.
Row 11: Work in pattern to end of row, picking up wraps and knitting them together with the sts they wrap.
Row 12: Repeat row 11.
Rows 13-15: finish working through Raglan shaping.

Work 6 rows in Garter st, then BO all sts loosely.

Finishing

Graft held stitches at the underarms and sew sleeve seams. Use yarn tails to close up any holes at the underarms.

Weave in ends, wash and block. Sew buttons over the buttonholes on whichever side you choose.

Bonnet Border Chart

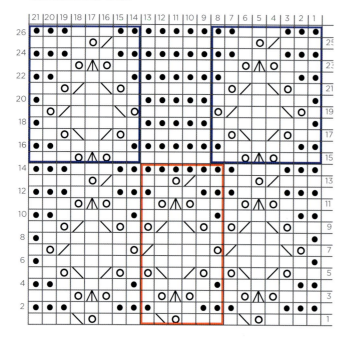

Edging Chart

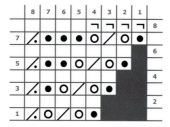

Legend:

☐ **knit**
RS: knit stitch
WS: purl stitch

O **yo**
RS: Yarn Over
WS: Yarn Over

◤ **ssk**
RS: Slip one stitch as if to knit, Slip another stitch as if to knit. Insert left-hand needle into front of these 2 stitches and knit them together
WS: Purl two stitches together in back loops, inserting needle from the left, behind and into the backs of the 2nd & 1st stitches in that order

• **purl**
RS: purl stitch
WS: knit stitch

▲ **Central Double Dec**
RS: Slip first and second stitches together as if to knit. Knit 1 stitch. Pass two slipped stitches over the knit stitch.
WS: Slip first and second stitches together as it to purl through the back loop. Purl 1 stitch. Pass two slipped stitches over the purl stitch.

◢ **k2tog**
RS: Knit two stitches together as one stitch
WS: Purl 2 stitches together

■ **No Stitch**
RS: Placeholder - No stitch made.

◢ **p2tog**
RS: Purl 2 stitches together
WS: Knit 2 stitches together

⌐ **Bind Off**

M **make one**
RS: Make one by lifting strand in between stitch just worked and thenext stitch, knit into back of this thread.
WS: Make one by lifting strand in between stitch just worked and thenext stitch, purl into back of this thread.

☐ border stitches

☐ pattern repeat

8 | Heirloom Layette Set

Sweater Border Chart

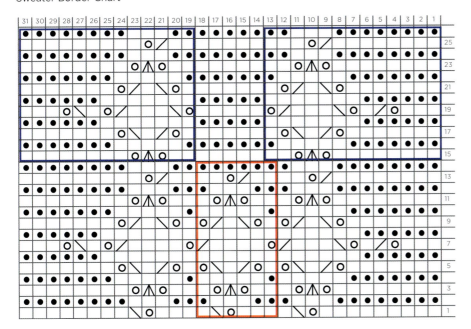

- border stitches
- pattern repeat

Sleeve Cuff Chart

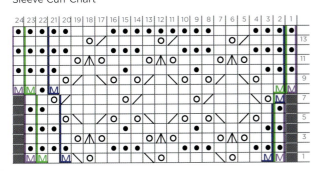

- Size 0
- Size 3 months
- Size 6 months

Sweater and Bonnet Schematics

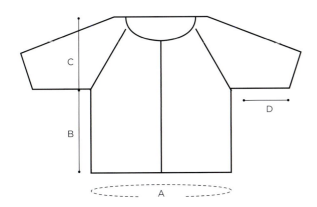

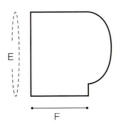

A 22.4 (23.3, 24.3)"
B 5.5 (5.8, 6.2")
C 3 (3.25, 3.4)"
D 6.3 (6.8, 7.3)"
E 10 (11, 12)"
F 4.6 (5.6, 6.6)"

Blanket Chart

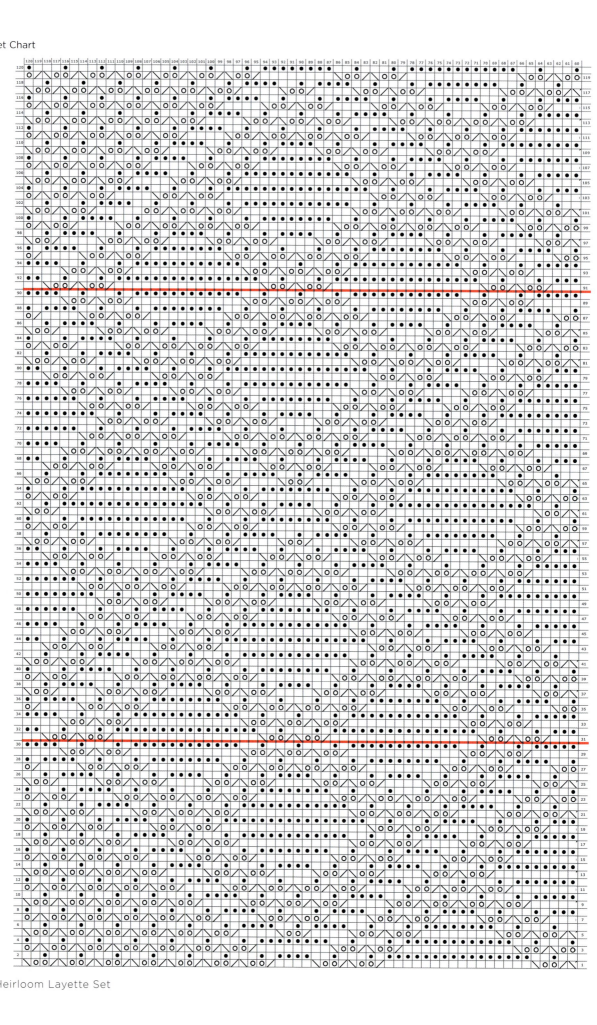

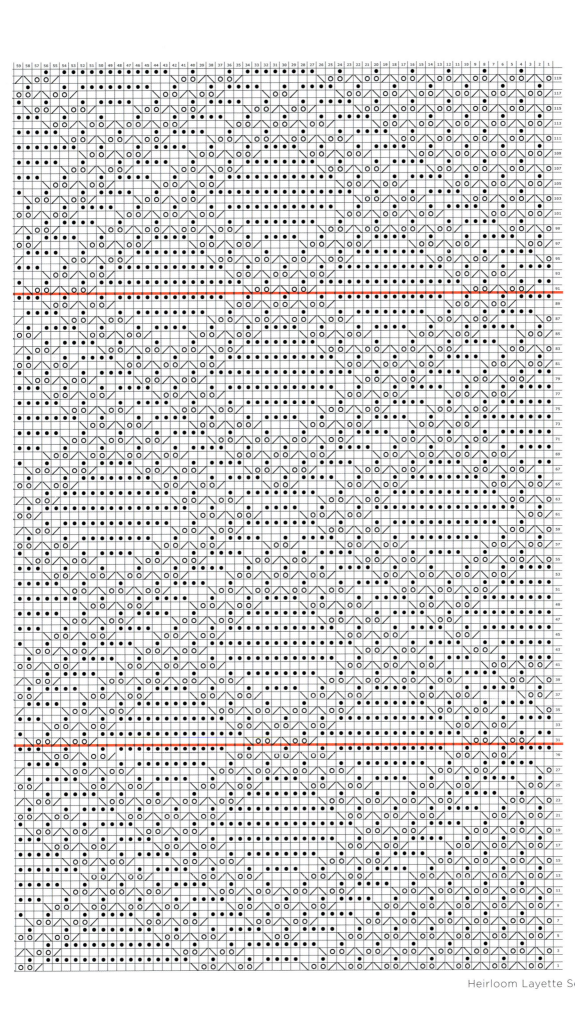

Heirloom Layette Set | 11

Next round: (K2tog, K1) three times, K1. 7 sts.
Next round: K2tog three times, K1. 4 sts.

Break yarn. With a yarn needle, pass the yarn tail through remaining live sts; pull tight to close hole.

Finishing

With Dogwood Heather, embroider the large Paw Pad design centered on the palms of the Mitts.

Sew a snap or Velcro dot to the tab and the wrist of the mitt. Sew a small decorative button on the top of the tab, above the snap or Velcro dot.

Weave in ends, wash and block.

Booties

The Booties begin at the center of the soles, and are then worked in the round up over the instep and ankle. Make two identically.

With Dove Heather, CO 28 (36, 32, 40) sts onto two DPNs or two sides of one circular needle using Judy's Magic Cast On. (14 (18, 16, 20) sts on each side.) Purl one round.

Round 2: K4, KFB, K to last 2 sts of that side, KFB, K1; on other side, K1, KFB, K to last 5 sts, KFB, K4. 4 sts increased.
Round 3: P3, PFB, P to last 4 sts of round, PFB, P3. 2 sts increased.
Round 4: K4, KFB, K to last 3 sts of that side, KFB, K2; on other side, K2, KFB, K to last 5 sts, KFB, K4. 4 sts increased.
Round 5: P3, PFB, P to last 4 sts of round, PFB, P3. 2 sts increased.
Round 6: K4, KFB, K to last 4 sts of that side, KFB, K3; on other side, K3, KFB, K to last 5 sts, KFB, K4. 4 sts increased.
Round 7: P3, PFB, P to last 4 sts of round, PFB, P3. 2 sts increased.
Round 8: K4, KFB, K to last 4 sts of that side, KFB, K3; on other side, K3, KFB, K to last 5 sts, KFB, K4. 4 sts increased.

Sizes 6 and 12 months: Repeat rounds 7-8 once more.

50 (58, 60, 68) sts on the needles.

Work around in Seed st for 8 (8, 10, 10) rounds.

Instep

On the next round, work in Seed st to 6 (6, 7, 7) sts before the end of the first side. With a spare DPN, work the next 12 (12, 14, 14) sts across the toe from row 1 of the Instep chart. You will now be working across the instep flat, attaching it to the sides of the foot.

To work instep rows: Slip the first st; work to the last st on the DPN following Instep chart. Work the last st of chart together with the next live st of the foot. Turn work.

Work across instep rows as shown for your size in the chart. When there are 9 (11, 11, 12) sts remaining on either side of the instep sts, begin working in the round: On the next RS row, work across the instep sts, but do not work a decrease; instead, continue working from Instep chart to the end of the round. There are now 30 (34, 36, 38) sts on the needles.

Continue working around the leg of the bootie, following the Instep chart, until the last round shown for your size. Work five rounds of Seed Stitch; BO all sts loosely.

Repeat for second bootie.

Finishing

With Dogwood Heather, embroider the small Paw Pad design to the soles, near the toes of the booties.

Weave in ends, wash and block.

Chevron Stripe

Back of Mitt

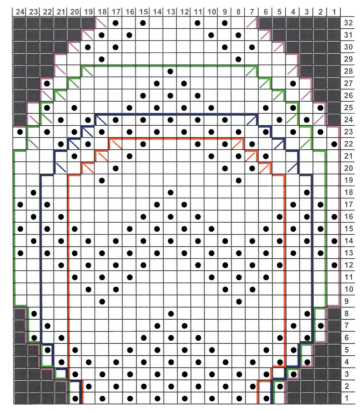

Chart is read bottom to top from right to left.

Begin working on Round 1 or Round 2 of the chart, depending on which round keeps the seed stitch patterning in line.

Where the pattern increases, work a KFB increase on either side..

Work decreases as shown.

Paw Pad Embroidery

Use the small paw (1") as a size guide for embroidering the booties, and the large paw (1.5") as a guide for the mitts.

Legend:

■ **No Stitch** — Placeholder - No stitch made.

□ **knit** — knit stitch

⊡ **purl** — purl stitch

╱ **K2tog** — If the symbol appears over a knit st in the chart, K2tog. If it occurs over a purl stitch in the chart, P2tog. K2tog on palm side of mitt.

╲ **SSK** — If the symbol appears over a knit st in the chart, SSK. If it occurs over a purl stitch in the chart, SSP. SSK on palm side of mitt.

— 0 months
— 3 months
— 6 months
— 12 months

Kitty Hat, Booties & Mitts Set

Instep

Kitty Hat, Booties & Mitts Set

LITTLE OLD MAN JACKET

by Kerin Dimeler-Laurence

FINISHED MEASUREMENTS
6 mos (12 mos, 18 mos, 2T, 3T, 4T)
10.8 (11.1, 11.4, 12.5, 12.8, 13.4)" Chest Width

YARN
Knit Picks Comfy Worsted (75% Pima Cotton, 25% Acrylic; 109 yards/50g): Doe 24797, 4 (4, 4, 4, 5, 5) balls.

NEEDLES
US 7 (4.5 mm) straights and DPNs or long circular needles for Magic Loop technique, or size to obtain gauge

NOTIONS
Yarn Needle
Stitch Markers
1 Locking Stitch Marker
Scrap yarn or Stitch Holder
12 ½" buttons

GAUGE
19 sts and 28 rows = 4" in St st worked flat.

Little Old Man Jacket

Notes:
This sweet unisex jacket features textured elbow patches and a double-breasted, shawl collared closure. It's just like grandpa's favorite cardigan, only much smaller!

Twisted Rib (in the round, over an even number of sts):
Every round: (K1 TBL, P1) around.

Twisted Rib (worked flat, over an even number of sts):
RS: (K1 TBL, P1) across row.
WS: (K1, P1 TBL) across row.

M1L (Make 1 Left-leaning stitch): PU the bar between st just worked and next st and place on LH needle mounted as a regular knit stitch; knit through the back of the loop.

M1R (Make 1 Right-leaning stitch): PU the bar between st just worked and next st and place on LH needle backwards (incorrect stitch mount). Knit through the front of the loop.

Three Needle Bind Off:
Hold the two pieces of knitting together with the points of the needles facing to the right. Insert a third needle into the first stitch on each of the needles knitwise, starting with the front needle. Work a knit stitch, pulling the loop through both of the stitches you've inserted the third needle through. After you've pulled the loop through, slip the first stitch off of each of the needles. This takes two stitches (one from the front needle and one from the back) and joins them to make one finished stitch on the third needle (held in your right hand). Repeat this motion, inserting your needle into one stitch on the front and back needles, knitting them together and slipping them off of the needles. Each time you complete a second stitch, pass the first finished stitch over the second and off of the needle (as you would in a traditional bind-off).
WS: (K1, P1 TBL) across row.

DIRECTIONS
Sleeves
Make two sleeves. Increases and Elbow Patches are worked at the same time; read both sections before proceeding.

With MC, CO 32 (34, 36, 36, 38, 38) sts. PM and join to work in the round, being careful not to twist sts. Work in Twisted Rib for 1.5 (1.5, 1.5, 2, 2, 2)".

Increases
Increase Round: K1, M1L, knit to last st, M1R, K1. 2 sts increased.

Begin working in Stockinette St. Work an increase round every 3rd (3rd, 4th, 4th, 4th, 4th) round 8 (10, 10, 11, 11, 12) times total. Work 4 (5, 3, 0, 0, 0) rounds in pattern. 48 (54, 56, 58, 60, 62) sts on the needles.

Elbow Patches
The elbow patches are little areas of seed st worked over the elbow area on each sleeve. On the left sleeve the patch is towards the beginning of the round, and on the right it's toward the end.

On the 7 (10, 14, 18, 20, 22) round of the sleeve, work 7 sts for Left sleeve (18 sts before end of round for Right sleeve). PM and begin working from Elbow patch chart over the next 11 sts, working each round of the chart from right to left; work in pattern to end of round. After all 15 rounds of the Elbow Patch have been worked remove marker, continue the sleeve in St st as established.

Sleeve Cap
On the next round, BO sts for the sleeve cap: Knit to 2 (3, 2, 3, 2, 3) sts before the end of the round. BO the last 2 (3, 2, 3, 2, 3) sts of this round and the first 3 (4, 2, 3, 3, 4) sts of the next, removing beg of rnd marker. K to last 2 sts of row, SSK. 42 (46, 48, 50, 52, 54) sts.

Decrease Row: K2tog or P2tog TBL over the first two sts of row; work in pattern to last 2 sts, SSK or P2tog. 1 st removed at each edge.

Work a Decrease Row every row 4 (5, 5, 6, 6, 7) times, then every other row 7 (5, 6, 7, 7, 8) times. 20 (26, 26, 36, 34, 30) sts. Work a Decrease Row every row 2 (5, 5, 2, 3, 2) times.

On the next row, decrease 2 sts at each end (K3tog and SSSK if a RS row, P3tog and SSSP if a WS row). BO remaining 12 (12, 12, 16, 16, 16) sts.

Body
The body is worked simply with buttonholes worked on both front flaps. When sewing on buttons, sew them over the holes opposite the side you'd like to use as the buttonhole side.

CO 132 (136, 140, 148, 152, 160) sts. Work in Garter st (knit every row) for 6 rows. On the next (RS) row, set up body: K20, PM to mark edge of front band, K 18 (19, 20, 22, 23, 25), PM to mark right underarm, K 56 (58, 60, 64, 66, 70), PM to mark left underarm, K 18 (19, 20, 22, 23, 25), PM to mark edge of front band, K to end. For the rest of the body, the front bands are worked in Garter st and the rest of the body in St st.

Buttonhole Row: Over the 20 sts of each front band, *K3, K2tog, YO twice, SSK, K3*, repeat between *s. Work the rest of the body in St st. On the next row, (K1, P1) into each double YO.

Work a Buttonhole Row on the next row, then every 8th (8th, 8th, 9th, 9th, 10th) row four times. Place a locking stitch marker through any stitch of the last buttonhole row to help you determine when to begin the armholes.

From here, both the Collar and Armholes are worked at the same time; read both sections before proceeding.

Armholes
On the 4th (8th, 8th, 9th, 11th, 12th) row after the last Buttonhole Row (marked with a locking marker), bind off sts at the underarms and work the fronts and back separately:

Work in pattern to 2 (2, 2, 3, 3, 3) sts before underarm marker. BO the next 4 (4, 4, 6, 6, 6) sts, removing marker. Repeat between *s once more; work in pattern to end.

Place the remaining 52 (54, 56, 58, 60, 64) Back sts on a holder or scrap yarn and continue working fronts with separate balls of yarn.

Armhole Decrease Row, RS: K1, K2tog over first 3 sts of Left front, work to last 3 sts of Right front, SSK, K1.
Armhole Decrease Row, WS: P1, SSP over first 3 sts of Right front, work to last 3 sts of Left front, P2tog, P1.

Work an Armhole Decrease Row on the next 3 (3, 3, 3, 4, 4) rows, then every other row 3 (2, 2, 3, 3, 4) times. A total of 6 (5, 5, 7, 7, 8) sts removed from each armhole edge.

Continue fronts, following remaining Collar and Shoulder directions.

Collar and Shoulders

On the next RS row after the last Buttonhole Row, begin collar shaping: KFB, work in pattern to last st, KFB. There are now 21 sts across each front band. Repeat this row every 4th row 4 more times. 25 sts across each front band.

Work front bands in Garter st and shoulders in St st for 0 (6, 8, 8, 8, 9) rows. Work front bands in Garter st and shoulders in Twisted Rib for 15 (17, 17, 17, 20, 20) rows. Place the 10 (12, 13, 12, 13, 14) shoulder sts on each side on st markers or scrap yarn.

Collar Extensions

The collar is continued and joined at the back neck. Both sides are worked the same.

Attach yarn to either side of collar; work in Garter st for 2.25". Place sts on a holder and repeat on other side.

Place both sets of sts on needles. With the RS of each facing, work a 3-needle BO over all sts. This seam should be hidden under the collar when it is folded over in the back.

Back

Back Armhole Decrease Row (RS): K1, K2tog, K to last 3 sts, SSK, K1.
Back Armhole Decrease Row (WS): P1, P2tog, P to last 3 sts, SSP, P1.

Place 52 (54, 56, 58, 60, 64) Back sts back on the needles. Attach yarn, ready to begin a WS row. Work a Back Armhole Decrease Row on the next 3 (3, 3, 3, 4, 4) rows, then every other row 3 (2, 2, 3, 3, 4) times. 40 (44, 46, 46, 46, 48) sts remain across Back. Work 3 (7, 9, 6, 3, 1) rows in St st.

Work 14 (16, 16, 16, 19, 19) rows in Twisted Rib. On the next row, work in Twisted Rib for 10 (12, 13, 12, 13, 14) sts, BO the next 20 (20, 20, 22, 20, 20) sts, work in Twisted Rib to end.

Faux Pockets

Cute little faux pocket flaps are picked up on the body and held in place with buttons.

Along the 16th (16th, 16th, 18th, 18th, 20th) row of St st on the body, count 5 (5, 6, 6, 7, 7) sts from the edge of each front band; place a marker through the next st. Count 9 (9, 9, 9, 11, 11) sts over from this marker and place another marker. PU and work in Twisted Rib across the 9 (9, 9, 9, 11, 11) sts between markers. Work in Twisted rib for 2 rows.

Row 3 (RS): K2tog, work in Twisted rib to last 2 sts, SSK.
Row 4 (WS): P2tog, work in Twisted rib to last 2 sts, SSP.
Row 5: Repeat row 3. BO all sts in pattern.

Finishing

Turn sweater inside out. Place matching Back and Front Shoulder sts back on the needles, so that both sets are held parallel. Work a 3-needle BO over all shoulder sts. Repeat on other shoulder.

Set in Sleeves

With right sides facing out, set sleeves into armhole openings, making sure that the center of each sleeve cap is placed at the shoulder seam and that BO sts under the sleeve and armhole are centered. Pin in place. Using yarn needle and yarn, begin at the underarm and sew sleeves into the armholes, using mattress stitch.

Collar

With the RS of the Back facing, line up the Collar Extension with the BO sts of the back neck, folding the Collar Extension to the inside of the sweater. Whipstitch the Collar Extension to the back neck.

Sew buttons opposite the buttonholes you wish to use; sew the other holes shut with the yarn tails from the buttons.

Fold the Pocket Flaps down towards the bottom of the sweater. Position a button in the center of each; sew the button on through both layers of fabric.

Weave in ends, wash and block.

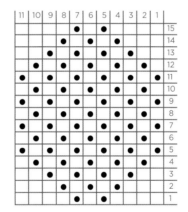

Legend:
- knit / knit stitch
- purl / purl stitch

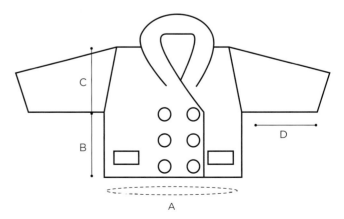

A 23.6 (24.4, 25.25, 26.9, 27.8, 29.5)"
B 6.25 (6.7, 6.7, 7.4, 7.7, 8.3)"
C 5 (5.7, 6, 6, 6.4, 6.6)"
D 5.4 (6.3, 7.7, 8.3, 8.3, 8.9)"

PETER & WENDY

by Kerin Dimeler-Laurence

FINISHED MEASUREMENTS
6 mos (12 mos, 18mos, 2T, 3T, 4T)
21.5 (21.5, 24, 24, 26.75, 26.75)" chest circumference

YARN
Knit Picks Swish DK (100% Superwash Merino Wool; 123 yards/50g):
Vest – Marina 25578, 2 (2, 3, 3, 3, 3) balls
Pinafore – Honey 26061, 4 (4, 4, 5, 5, 6) balls

NEEDLES
US 6 (4 mm) 16" circular needles, or size to obtain gauge

NOTIONS
Yarn Needle
Stitch Markers
Scrap yarn or Stitch Holders
Two 1" Buttons, each
Cable Needle

GAUGE
24 sts and 32 rows = 4" in Baby Cable pattern worked in the round, blocked.

Peter & Wendy

Notes:
Sweet and simple, this little vest or pinafore is as warm as it is cute. The vest and pinafore are knit from the bottom up in the round, then worked flat across the chest and back. Button tabs extend from the back over the shoulders, making this an easy-on, easy-off garment.

CDD (centered double decrease):
Slip two stitches to the RH needle as if to K2tog. Knit the next stitch, then pass two slipped sts over; two sts removed.

SSSP - slip, slip, slip, purl (left slanting double decrease): Holding yarn in front, slip three stitches knitwise one at a time to right needle. Slip them back onto left needle and purl the three stitches together through the back loops—three stitches reduced to one. (It looks the same as an SSSK on the RS)

DIRECTIONS
Vest
CO 128 (128, 144, 144, 160, 160) sts. PM and join to work in the round, being careful not to twist sts. Work in Garter Stitch (knit one round, purl one round) for 16 rounds.

Begin working from Baby Cable chart on round 5, repeating these 8 sts 16 (16, 18, 18, 20, 20) times around the body. After reaching round 8, work 5 (5, 5, 6, 6, 7) more 8-round repeats. On the last round, place a marker after 64 (64, 72, 72, 80, 80) sts to mark the right underarm. Move on to Armhole Shaping directions.

Pinafore
CO 160 (176, 198, 216, 220, 240) sts. PM and join to work in the round, being careful not to twist sts. Work in Garter Stitch (knit one round, purl one round) for 16 rounds.

On the next round, begin pattern: *P 1(2, 2, 2, 2, 2), work across Baby Cable chart on round 1, P 1 (1, 1, 2, 1, 2), PM*. Repeat between *s 16 (16, 18, 18, 20, 20) times around.

Sizes 18 mos (3T): Work one (two) 8-round repeat(s), working the extra purl sts between stitch repeats as established.

All sizes: Work through round 7 of the Baby Cable chart, working the extra purl sts between stitch repeats as established. On the next round, begin decreases.

Decreases
The decreases in the skirt of the pinafore are staggered, giving it a smooth A-line shape. Decrease rounds always occur over the 8th round of the Baby Cable pattern.

Left Decrease, Odd (LO): Work through stitch 6 of the first repeat of the Baby Cable pattern, P2tog, work to end of repeat. Repeat this on the 3rd, 5th, 7th repeats, and so on across the round. 8 (8, 9, 9, 10, 10) sts removed.

Left Decrease, Even (LE): Work through stitch 6 of the second repeat of the Baby Cable pattern, P2tog, work to end of repeat. Repeat this on the 4th, 6th, 8th repeats, and so on across the round. 8 (8, 9, 9, 10, 10) sts removed.

Right Decrease, Odd (RO): Over the first two sts of the first repeat of the Baby Cable pattern, P2tog, work to end of repeat. Repeat this on the 3rd, 5th, 7th repeats, and so on across the round. 8 (8, 9, 9, 10, 10) sts removed.

Right Decrease, Even (RE): Over the first two sts of the second repeat of the Baby Cable pattern, P2tog, work to end of repeat. Repeat this on the 4th, 6th, 8th repeats, and so on across the round. 8 (8, 9, 9, 10, 10) sts removed.

All sizes: Work the next round (round 8 of the Baby Cable chart) with RO (Right Decrease, Odd) instructions.

6 mos: Work two 8-round repeats in pattern, work LE instructions on next repeat, work two 8-round repeats in pattern, work RE instructions on next repeat, work two 8-round repeats in pattern, work LO instructions on next repeat. 2 sts decreased from each repeat; 128 sts remain.

12 mos (18 mos, 3T): Work one 8-round repeat in pattern, work RE instructions on next repeat, work one 8-round repeat in pattern, work LO instructions on next repeat, work one 8-round repeat in pattern, work RO instructions on next repeat, work one 8-round repeat in pattern, work LE instructions on next repeat, work one 8-round repeat in pattern, work RE instructions on next repeat. 3 sts decreased from each repeat; 128 (144, 160) sts remain. 3T only: work one 8-round repeat in pattern.

2T: Work one 8-round repeat in pattern, work LE instructions on next repeat, work one 8-round repeat in pattern, work RE instructions on next repeat, work one 8-round repeat in pattern, work LO instructions on next repeat, work one 8-round repeat in pattern, work RO instructions on next repeat, work one 8-round repeat in pattern, work LE instructions on next repeat, work one 8-round repeat in pattern, work RE instructions on next repeat, work one 8-round repeat in pattern, work LO instructions on next repeat. 4 sts decreased from each repeat; 144 sts remain.

4T: Work one 8-round repeat in pattern, work LE instructions on next repeat, work one 8-round repeat in pattern, work RE instructions on next repeat, work one 8-round repeat in pattern, work LO instructions on next repeat, work one 8-round repeat in pattern, work RO instructions on next repeat, work one 8-round repeat in pattern, work LE instructions on next repeat, work one 8-round repeat in pattern, work RE instructions on next repeat, work one 8-round repeat in pattern, work LO instructions on next repeat. 4 sts decreased from each repeat; 160 sts remain.

All sizes: Work one 8-round repeat in pattern. On the final round, remove pattern repeat markers and place a marker after 80 (88, 99, 108, 110, 120) sts to mark the right underarm. Move on to Armhole Shaping.

Armhole Shaping (Vest and Pinafore)
On the next round, begin the shaping for the armholes. The armholes and neckline are worked at the same time, so be sure to read both sections before continuing. The Neckline shaping begins 5 (5, 7, 5, 7, 7) rows after the armhole borders are cast on.

Both the armholes and neckline are bordered in Garter stitch that is cast on and then knit with the body. The curving decreases shape the borders into gentle shapes with little seaming involved.

BO round: Work in pattern to 1 (1, 2, 2, 2, 2) sts before right underarm marker. BO the next 2 (2, 4, 4, 4, 4) sts, removing marker. Work in pattern to 1 (1, 2, 2, 2, 2) sts before the end of the round; BO the next 1 (1, 2, 2, 2, 2) sts and the first 1 (1, 2, 2, 2, 2) sts of the next round, removing marker.

Place the 62 (62, 68, 68, 76, 76) Back sts on a stitch holder or scrap yarn.

Across the front, SSK, pass the first knit st (last of the bound off sts) over, decreasing 2 *work in pattern to the last 3 sts, K3tog. PM and cast on 5 sts directly after the last st. Turn and knit across the first 5 sts, SM, P2tog (P2tog, P2tog, P2tog, P3tog, P3tog), work in pattern across the WS, knitting the knits and purling the purls, to the last 2 (2, 2, 2, 3, 3) sts; SSP (SSP, SSP, SSP, SSSP, SSSP). PM and cast on 5 sts after the last st. 66 (66, 72, 72, 78, 78) sts on the needles.

Decrease row (RS): K5, SM, if the second st on the LH needle is a knit st, SSK, if a purl st, SSP; work in pattern to 2 sts before next marker; if the next st is a knit st, K2tog, if a purl st, P2tog, SM, K5.

Decrease row (WS): K5, SM, if the second st on the LH needle is a knit st, K2tog, if a purl st, P2tog; work in pattern to 2 sts before next marker; if the next st is a knit st, SSK, if a purl st, SSP, SM, K5.

Continue working the 5 sts at each edge in Garter stitch and working in pattern across the front, decreasing as follows: Work a decrease row on the next 2 (1, 1, 1, 4, 3) rows, then every other row 1 (1, 3, 1, 2, 3) times; work 4 (4, 2, 3, 3, 2) rows in pattern, work a decrease row, work 5 (5, 3, 5, 4, 4) rows in pattern, work a decrease row. 10 (8, 12, 8, 16, 16) sts removed from the Front.

Continue in pattern, working the armhole sides with no further decreases over the remaining 22 (28, 31, 32, 36, 36) rows of the Front.

Neckline

5 (5, 7, 5, 7, 7) rows after casting on the second Armhole border, bind off for the neckline.

Count the number of stitches on the Front, and mark the center. Work in pattern to one st before the center and BO 2 sts. Continue across row, following armhole decreases. On the next row, work in pattern to 2 sts before first bound off st. If the next st is a purl st, P2tog, if the next st is a knit st, SSK. PM and CO 5 sts after the last st to begin neck band.

With a second ball of yarn, CO 5 sts, PM and begin working across the other side of the Front: If the second st on the LH needle is a purl st, SSP; if it is a K st, K2tog. Continue in pattern across front.

Neckline Decrease row: At the left (as knit) neckline edge, K2tog the last body pattern st together with the first st of the neckline border; at right (as knit) neckline edge, SSK the last st of the neckline border with the first body st.

Work a Neckline Decrease Row every row 5 (6, 5, 6, 4, 4) times, then every other row 6 (5, 7, 6, 4, 4) times, then every third row 0 (3, 0, 2, 2, 2) times, then every 4th row 2 (0, 2, 2, 4, 4) times. 15 (15, 16, 16, 17, 17) sts remain on each shoulder.

Work in pattern for 0 (5, 4, 1, 5, 5) rows. Work in Garter st across all sts for 6 rows.

Next row: K2tog, K to last 2 sts, SSK.
Next row: K3tog, BO to the last 3 sts, SSSK, pass last BO st over. BO remaining st.

Back

Place 62 (62, 68, 68, 76, 76) Back sts back on the needles. Attach yarn, ready to work a RS row. K3tog, begin working from * in Front armhole directions. Work through armhole shaping, as done for Front; 56 (58, 60, 64, 62, 62) sts remain. Work in pattern for 10 (16, 16, 17, 19, 19) rows. On the next row, knit across all sts; work Back in Garter st (knit every row) for another 10 (10, 13, 13, 15, 15) rows.

On the next row, BO neckline: K 15 (15, 16, 16, 17, 17), BO the next 26 (28, 28, 32, 28, 28) sts. Knit to end.

Shoulders

Work both Back Shoulders identically (work them at the same time if you wish). These shoulders will extend as tabs over the front to fasten to the buttons.

Work in Garter st for 1 (1.5, 2, 2, 2.5, 2.5)". On the next row, make a buttonhole: K6 (6, 6, 6, 7, 7), BO 3 sts, K6 (6, 7, 7, 7, 7). Turn and knit, casting on three new sts over the bound off sts. Knit one row.

Begin decreases:
Row 1: K2tog, K to last 2 sts, SSK.
Row 2: Knit.
Rows 3-6: Repeat rows 1-2.
Row 7: K2tog, K to last 2 sts, SSK.
Row 8: Repeat row 7. 5 (5, 6, 6, 7, 7) sts remain.

Sizes 6 mos (12 mos):
Row 9: K2tog, K1, SSK.
Row 10: CDD. BO remaining st.

Sizes 18 mos (2T):
Row 9: K3tog, SSSK.
Row 10: Pass 1st st over 2nd to BO. BO remaining st.

Sizes 3T (4T):
Row 9: K3tog, K1, SSSK.
Row 10: CDD. BO remaining st.

Finishing

Graft armhole borders together at underarms; graft neckline border up the center neck.

Weave in ends. Sew buttons to front shoulders about 1" below bind off. Wash and block.

Baby Cable Chart

Chart is worked in the round and read bottom to top from right to left

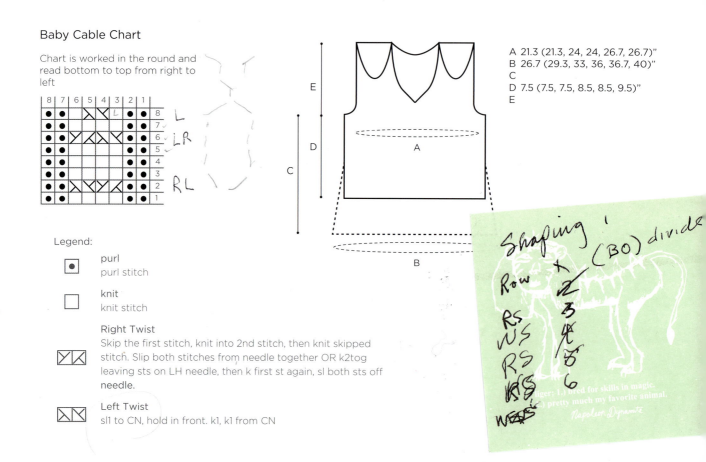

Legend:

- ⊡ **purl** — purl stitch
- ☐ **knit** — knit stitch
- ⋈ **Right Twist** — Skip the first stitch, knit into 2nd stitch, then knit skipped stitch. Slip both stitches from needle together OR k2tog leaving sts on LH needle, then k first st again, sl both sts off needle.
- ⋈ **Left Twist** — sl1 to CN, hold in front. k1, k1 from CN

A 21.3 (21.3, 24, 24, 26.7, 26.7)"
B 26.7 (29.3, 33, 36, 36.7, 40)"
C
D 7.5 (7.5, 7.5, 8.5, 8.5, 9.5)"
E

Legend:

- ● purl — purl stitch
- ☐ knit — knit stitch
- ⋈ Right Twist — Skip the first stitch, knit into 2nd stitch, then knit skipped stitch. Slip both stitches from needle together OR k2tog leaving sts on LH needle, then k first st again, sl both sts off needle.
- ⋈ Left Twist — sl1 to CN, hold in front, k1, k1 from CN
- ■ No Stitch — Placeholder – No stitch made.

Peter & Wendy | 29

SLEEPY KITTY STUFFED TOY

by Kerin Dimeler-Laurence

FINISHED MEASUREMENTS
12" long body

YARN
Knit Picks Comfy Sport (75% Pima Cotton, 25% Acrylic; 136 yards/50g): Parchment 25764, Ivory 24429, 2 balls each, Flamingo 24426, 1 ball.

NEEDLES
US 3 (3.25 mm) straight and DPNs or circular needles, or size to obtain gauge

NOTIONS
Yarn Needle
Stitch Markers
5 Locking Ring Markers
Scrap Yarn or Stitch Holders
Crochet Hook and smooth scrap yarn for provisional CO
Dark brown embroidery floss or fine yarn
Fiber fill stuffing

GAUGE
24 sts and 34 rows = 4" in St st, worked flat, blocked.

Sleepy Kitty Stuffed Toy

Notes:
This adorable friend is worked in pieces and assembled.

Provisional Cast On (Crochet Chain Method)
Using a crochet hook several sizes too big for the yarn, make a slipknot and chain for 1". Hold knitting needle in left hand. With yarn in back of the needle, work next chain st by pulling the yarn over the needle and through the chain st. Move yarn under and behind needle, and repeat for the number of sts required. Chain a few more sts off the needle, then break yarn and pull end through last chain. CO sts will be incorrectly mounted; knit into the back of these sts. To unravel (when sts need to be picked up), pull chain end out, and the chain should unravel, leaving live sts.

Wrap and Turn
Work until the stitch to be wrapped. If knitting: Bring yarn to the front of the work, slip next st as if to purl, return the yarn to the back; turn work and slip wrapped st onto RH needle. Continue across row. If purling: Bring yarn to the back of the work, slip next st as if to purl, return the yarn to the front; turn work and slip wrapped st onto RH needle. Continue across row.

Picking up wraps: Work to the wrapped st. If knitting, insert the RH needle under the wrap(s), then through the wrapped st kwise. Knit the wrap(s) together with the wrapped st. If purling, slip the wrapped st pwise onto the RH needle, and use the LH needle to lift the wrap(s) and place them on the RH needle. Slip wrap(s) and unworked st back to LH needle; purl all together through the back loop.

CDD (Centered Double Decrease)
Slip two stitches to the RH needle as if to K2tog. Knit the next stitch, then pass two slipped sts over; two sts removed.

DIRECTIONS
Body
The body is knit flat and seamed to give shape.

With scrap yarn, provisionally CO 30 sts. With Parchment, K 1 row, placing markers after 5 and 25 sts. Purl 1 row.

Join Ivory. Work Rows 1-60 alternating two rows of Ivory with two rows of Parchment. Carry unused color up the side of work.

Row 1: K1, M1L, K to first marker, M1R, SM, K to M, SM, M1L, K to last st, M1R, K1. 34 sts.
Row 2: P1, M1L Pwise, purl to last st, M1R Pwise, P1. 36 sts.
Row 3-8: Repeat rows 1-2. 54 sts.
Row 9: K1, M1L, K to last st, M1R, K1. 56 sts.
Row 10: P1, M1L Pwise, purl to last st, M1R Pwise, P1. 58 sts.
Row 11: K1, M1L, K to first marker, M1R, SM, K to M, SM, M1L, K to last st, M1R, K1. 62 sts.
Row 12: Repeat row 10. 64 sts.
Row 13: K1, M1L, K to last st, M1R, K1. 66 sts.
Row 14: Purl.
Rows 15-16: Repeat rows 13-14. 68 sts.
Row 17: Knit.
Row 18: Purl.
Row 19-20: Repeat rows 13-14. 70 sts.
Rows 21-24: Repeat rows 17-20. 72 sts.
Rows 25-32: Work in Stockinette st.
Row 33: K2tog, knit to last 2 sts, SSK. 70 sts. Place a locking ring marker through any stitch in this row; this will be used for assembly.
Row 34: Purl.
Row 35: K3tog, K to last 3 sts, SSSK. 66 sts.
Row 36: P2tog, P to last 2 sts, SSP. 64 sts.
Row 37: K2tog, K to 2 sts before M, SSK, SM, K to M, SM, K2tog, K to last 2 sts, SSK. 60 sts.
Row 38: Repeat row 36. 58 sts.
Rows 39-40: Repeat rows 37-38. 52 sts.
Row 41: K to first M, SM, SSK, K to 2 sts before next M, K2tog, K to end. 50 sts. Place a locking ring marker through any stitch in this row; this will be used for assembly.
Row 42: Purl.
Row 43: K to 2 sts before M, SSK, SM, K to M, SM, K2tog, K to end. 48 sts.
Row 44: Purl.
Rows 45-48: Repeat rows 41-44. 44 sts.
Row 49-50: Repeat rows 43-44. 42 sts.
Row 51: K1, M1L, K1, M1L, K to 2 sts before marker, SSK, SM, K to marker, SM, K2tog, K to last 2 sts, M1R, K1, M1R, K1. 44 sts.
Row 52: P1, M1L Pwise, P to last st, M1R Pwise, P1. 46 sts.
Rows 53-56: Repeat rows 51-52. 54 sts.
Row 57-58: Repeat rows 43-44. 52 sts.
Row 59: K to M, SM, K2tog, K to 2 sts before M, SSK, SM, K to end. 50 sts.
Row 60: Purl. 18 sts each side, 14 center sts.

Place sts on scrap yarn or stitch holder and work Belly.

Belly
The Belly portion is picked up and knit and sewn onto the body. Short rows shape the rump, and the back feet are added like gussets for mitten thumbs.

Unravel the Provisional CO and place the 30 sts on needles. With RS facing, attach Ivory and K 1 row.

Row 1 (WS): Purl 20, W&T.
Row 2 (RS): K10, W&T.
Row 3: P10, PU wrap, W&T.
Row 4: K11, PU wrap, W&T.
Row 5: P12, PU wrap, W&T.
Row 6: K13, PU wrap, K2tog, turn.
Row 7: Sl 1, P14, PU wrap, P2tog, turn.
Row 8: Sl 1, K15, SSK, turn.
Row 9: Sl 1, P15, P2tog, turn.
Rows 10-17: Repeat rows 8-9.
Row 18: Sl 1, K15, SSK, turn.
Row 19: Sl 1, purl to end.
Row 20: Sl 1, knit to end.
Rows 21-26: Repeat rows 19-20.
Row 27: Repeat row 19. 17 sts.

Back Feet

On the next row, the back feet are begun like thumb gussets.

Row 28: K2, PM, knit into the front, back, and front of the next st, PM, K to last 3 sts, PM, knit into the front, back, and front of the next st, PM, K2. 4 sts increased, 21 sts.

Row 29: P2, *SM, M1L Pwise, P to M, M1R Pwise, SM*, P to M, repeat between *s, P2. 2 sts increased between markers, 4 total. 25 sts.

Row 30: K2, *SM, M1L, K to M, M1R, SM*, K to M, repeat between *s, K2. 29 sts.

Rows 31-32: Repeat rows 29-30. 37 sts.

Row 33: Purl.

Row 34: Repeat row 30. 41 sts.

Rows 35-36: Repeat rows 33-34. 45 sts.

Row 37: Purl.

Row 38: Knit.

Rows 39-40: Repeat rows 33-34. 49 sts.

Rows 41-43: Work in St st.

On the next row (RS), place the back feet on holders to be continued later: K2, *slip next 16 sts onto scrap yarn or a stitch holder, removing markers. CO 3 sts after last st worked, and join to body by knitting into next live st.* Knit to next marker and repeat between *s, K to end. 23 sts.

Rows 45-51: Work in St st. Place a locking stitch marker through any stitch in the last row; this is a marker that will be used when seaming.

Row 52 (RS): K5, K2tog, K to last 7 sts, SSK, K5. 21 sts.

Row 53: Purl.

Row 54: K6, K2tog, K to last 8 sts, SSK, K6. 19 sts.

Row 55: Purl.

Row 56: K7, CDD, K to end. Place a locking stitch marker through any stitch in the last row; this is a marker that will be used when seaming. 17 sts.

Rows 57-64: Work in St st.

Row 65: Purl, placing a locking stitch through any stitch in the row; this is a marker that will be used when seaming.

On the next row, begin increases for front paws.

Row 66: K1, *PM, knit into the front, back and front of next st, PM*, K to last two sts, rep between *'s, K1. 4 sts increased, 21 sts.

Row 67: P1, *SM, M1L Pwise, P to marker, M1R Pwise, SM, * P to next M, repeat between *s, P1. 25 sts.

Row 68: K1, *SM, M1L, K to M, M1R, SM,* K to next M, repeat between *s, K1. 29 sts.

Rows 69-70: Repeat rows 67-68. 37 sts.

Row 71: Repeat row 67. 41 sts.

Row 72: K to 2nd M, M1R, SM, K to next M, SM, M1L, P to end. 43 sts.

Row 73: Purl to 3rd M. Place remaining 14 sts on scrap yarn or a stitch holder, removing markers. 29 sts.

Row 74: Knit to 1st marker. Place remaining 14 sts on scrap yarn or a stitch holder, removing markers. 15 sts.

Row 75: SSSP, Purl to last 2 sts, P3tog. 11 sts.

Row 76: K3tog, K to last 2 sts, SSSK. 7 sts.

These 7 sts will now be joined with the Body to work the neck and head in the round.

Neck

Slip first ten and last ten sts of the Body onto separate stitch holders or lengths of scrap yarn. Place remaining 30 Body sts back on the needles along with remaining 7 Belly sts, ready to begin a RS row. 37 sts. Ivory and Parchment will alternate every 3 rows.

Row 1: With Ivory, K 8, PM, K2tog, K 10, SSK, PM, K8, PM, K across 7 Belly sts, PM and join to work in the round. 35 sts.

Round 2: Knit to end.

The back of the head is now shaped with increases and short rows. PU wraps as you come to them.

Row 3: With Parchment, (K to st before M, M1R, K1, SM, K1, M1L) twice, K3, W&T. 39 sts.

Row 4: P to M, SM, P1, M1L Pwise, P to 1 st before M, M1R Pwise, P1, SM, P3, W&T. 41 sts.

Round 5: (K to st before M, M1R, K1, SM, K1, M1L) twice, K8, M1R, K7, M1L. 47 sts.

Row 6: With Ivory, (K to st before M, M1R, K1, SM, K1, M1L) twice, K2, W&T. 51 sts.

Row 7: P to 4 sts past 2nd marker, W&T.

Round 8: K to st before M, M1R, K1, SM, K to M, SM, K1, M1L, K7, M1R, K7, M1L, K1. 55 sts.

Row 9: With Parchment, K to st before M, M1R, K1, SM, K to M, SM, K1, M1L, K2, W&T. 57 sts.

Row 10: Repeat row 7.

Round 11: (K to st before M, M1R, K1, SM, K1, M1L) twice, K 13, M1R, K7, M1L, K2. 63 sts.

Row 12: With Ivory, (K to 1 st before M, M1R, K1, SM, K1, M1L) twice, K6, W&T. 67 sts.

Row 13: P 9 sts past 2nd M, W&T.

Round 14: K to 1 st before 1st M, M1R, K1, SM, K to next M, SM, K1, M1L, K16, M1R, K7, M1L, K3. 71 sts.

Row 15: With Parchment, K to 2 sts before 2nd M, W&T.

Row 16: P to 2 sts before M, W&T.

Row 17: K to 11 sts before end of round, M1R, K7, M1L, K4. 73 sts.

Round 18: With Ivory, K to 4 sts before M, W&T.

Row 19: P to 4 sts before M, W&T.

Row 20: K to 12 sts before end of row, M1R, K7, M1L, K5. 75 sts.

Round 21: With Parchment, K to 2 sts past 2nd M, W&T.

Row 22: P to 2 sts past 2nd M, W&T.

Row 23: K to 13 sts before end of row, M1R, K7, M1L, K6. 77 sts.

Round 25: With Ivory, K to 4 sts past 2nd M, W&T.

Row 26: P to 4 sts past 2nd M, W&T.

Row 27: K to end.

Round 28: With Parchment, K to 6 sts past 2nd M, W&T.

Row 29: P to 6 sts past 2nd M, W&T.

Row 30: K to end.

Round 31: With Ivory, K to 9 sts past 2nd M, W&T.

Row 32: P to 9 sts past 2nd M, W&T.

Row 33: K to end.

Round 34: With Parchment, K to 12 sts past 2nd M, W&T.

Row 35: P to 12 sts past 2nd M, W&T.

Row 36: K to end. Break Parchment.

Round 37: With Ivory, K to 15 sts past 2nd M, W&T.

Row 38: P to 15 sts past 2nd M, W&T.

Row 39: K to end.

Round 40: Knit to 4 sts before the first marker, PM to mark eye decrease, K10, removing existing marker, PM to mark forehead decrease, K to 6 sts before next marker, PM to mark forehead decrease, K10, removing existing marker, PM to mark eye decrease, K11, PM to mark mouth decrease (the other mouth decrease is the beginning of the round), K to end.
Round 41: K to 2 sts before first forehead marker, K2tog, SM, K to next forehead marker, SM, SSK, K to mouth marker, SM, K2tog, K to last 2 sts, SSK. 73 sts.
Round 42: K to 2 sts before first eye marker, K2tog, K to next eye marker, SM, SSK, K to end. 71 sts.
Rounds 43-44: Repeat rounds 41-42. 65 sts.
Round 45: K to 2 sts before first eye marker, K2tog, SM, K to 2 sts before first forehead marker, K2tog, SM, K to next forehead marker, SM, SSK, K to next eye marker, SM, SSK, K to mouth marker, SM, K2tog, K to last 2 sts, SSK. 59 sts.
Round 46: Repeat round 45. 53 sts.
Round 47: K to 2 sts before first eye marker, K2tog, SM, K to 3 sts before first forehead marker, K3tog, SM, K to next forehead marker, SM, SSSK, K to next eye marker, SM, SSK, K to mouth marker, SM, K3tog, K to last 3 sts, SSSK. 43 sts.
Round 48: K to K to 3 sts before first forehead marker, K3tog, SM, K2, K2tog, K4, SSK, K2, SM, SSSK, K to mouth marker, SM, K3tog, K to last 3 sts, SSSK. 33 sts.
Round 49: K to 2 sts before first eye marker, K2tog, SM, K2tog, remove forehead M, K1, SSK, K4, K2tog, K1, remove forehead M, SSK, SM, SSK, K to end. 27 sts.
Round 50: K5, K2tog, removing marker, K8, SSK, removing marker, K3, K2tog, removing marker, k to last st, SSK over the last st of this round and the first st of the next; move beg of rnd marker one st to the left. 23 sts.
Round 51: K4, SSK, K4, K2tog, K2, W&T. 21 sts.
Row 52: P12, W&T.
Round 53: K2, SSK, K4, K2tog, K to end. 19 sts.
Row 54: K 11, W&T.
Row 55: P2tog, P4, P2tog TBL, W&T. 17 sts.
Round 56: K7, K2tog, K to last st, SSK last st of round and first st of next row. 15 sts.
Round 57: K3, CDD, K4, CDD, K2. 11 sts.

Back Paws

The Back Paws are begun identically as little tapered tubes. Paw prints are embroidered on the toes.
Place the held sts of either back foot onto DPNs or circular needles. Attach Ivory, ready to begin a RS row, and knit across all 16 sts. Do not turn. PU and knit into the three cast on sts across the gap. PM and join to work in the round. 19 sts.

Work in St st in the round for 2".

Shape Right Paw:
Round 1: K4, K2tog, K4, SSK, K to end of round. 17 sts.
Round 2: Knit.
Round 3: K4, K2tog, K2, SSK, K to end of round. 15 sts.
Round 4: Knit.
Round 5: K1, SSK, K1, K2tog, SSK, K1, K2tog, K to end. 11 sts.
Round 6: SSK, K3, K2tog, K2, SSK. 8 sts.

Break yarn, leaving 12" tail. Arrange so that the first four sts of the round are on one needle, and the second four are on another. Using the yarn tail, graft the toe closed.

Shape Left Paw:
Round 1: K6, K2tog, K4, SSK, K to end of round. 17 sts.
Round 2: Knit.
Round 3: K6, K2tog, K2, SSK, K to end of round. 15 sts.
Round 4: Knit.
Round 5: K3, SSK, K1, K2tog, SSK, K1, K2tog, K2. 11 sts.
Round 6: K1, SSK, K3, K2tog, K1, SSK. 8 sts.

Knit the first two sts of the next round. Break yarn, leaving 12" tail. Arrange so that the next four sts of the round are on one needle, and the rest (including the two just knit) are on another. Using the yarn tail, graft the toe closed over these 8 sts.

Embroidering Paws
With Flamingo, embroider paw prints onto the fronts of the paws, centered with the decreases. Turn the paws inside out and fasten off the yarn ends on the wrong side of the work.

Tail
The tail is a simple tube worked in the round and stuffed.

With Parchment, CO 14 sts. Join to work in the round and PM, being careful not to twist sts. *Knit two rounds in Parchment, then two rounds in Ivory; repeat from * for 6". Break Parchment. With Ivory, knit 1" plain.
Next round: (K2, K2tog) three times, K2. 11 sts.
Next round: (K2tog, K1) three times, K2tog. 7 sts.
Last round: K2tog 3 times, K1.

Break yarn, leaving a 6" tail. With a yarn needle, pull the tail through the remaining live sts, and pull tight to close the hole.

Turn the Tail inside out. Weave in ends. Turn right side out and stuff lightly.

Assembly
Stuff the back feet. Through the open sides of the belly, stuff the body.

Line the belly up along the sides of the body. Match up the markers in row 33 of the body and row 51 of the belly. Using the markers, pin the body and belly together at the edges of these rows. Do the same with the markers in row 41 of the body and 56 of the belly. Pin the edges of the set-aside sts on body and belly for the forepaws so that the sts form a continuous row. With Ivory, and starting from row 19 of the belly, seam the two pieces together along both sides, evening out the fabric so that it does not gather. Stuff the body as you work up towards the head.

Forepaws

The forepaws are picked up and knit around using set-aside sts from both the body and belly.

Both paws: Place the 14 held sts from the belly and 10 sts from the body on the needles. Beginning close to the body, attach Ivory and knit all sts. PM and join to work in the round. Knit 15 rounds.

Shape Right Paw
Round 1: K2, SSK, K5, K2tog, K to end of rnd. 22 sts.
Round 2: K7, K2tog, K4, SSK, K to end. 20 sts.
Round 3: K2, SSK, K2, K2tog, K4, SSK, K2, K2tog, K2. 16 sts. At this point, you may stuff the paw.
Round 4: K4, K2tog, K4, SSK, K4. 14 sts.
Round 5: (K2, CDD, K2) twice: 10 sts.

Break yarn, leaving a 6" tail. Finish stuffing the paw. With a yarn needle and the yarn tail, graft the remaining sts closed. Weave in the end and bury in the paw.

Shape Left Paw
Round 1: K13, SSK, K5, K2tog, K to end of rnd. 22 sts.
Round 2: K7, K2tog, K4, SSK, K to end. 20 sts.
Round 3: K2, SSK, K2, K2tog, K4, SSK, K2, K2tog, K2. 16 sts. At this point, you may stuff the paw.
Round 4: K4, K2tog, K4, SSK, K4. 14 sts.
Round 5: (K2, CDD, K2) twice: 10 sts.

Break yarn, leaving a 6" tail. Finish stuffing the paw. With a yarn needle and the yarn tail, graft the remaining sts closed. Weave in the end and bury in the paw.

Embroidering Paws
With Flamingo, embroider paw prints onto the fronts of the paws, centered with the decreases. Weave in the end and bury in the paw.

Head

Finish stuffing Body and Head. K2tog around, K1. K2tog three times, draw yarn through remaining 3 sts to fasten off and bury end in body. Ears are knit separately and sewn on, and a sweet sleepy little face is embroidered.

Ears

The ears are knit separately and sewn on. Knit two identically.

With Ivory, CO 22 sts. PM and join to work in the round. Divide so that the first 10 sts are the front and next 12 sts the back. Knit three rounds.

Round 4: K1, K2tog, K4, SSK, K to end. 20 sts.
Round 5: Knit.
Round 6: K1, K2tog, K2, SSK, K2, K2tog, K6, SSK, K1. 16 sts.
Round 7: Knit.
Round 8: K1, K2tog, SSK, K2, K2tog, K4, SSK, K1. 12 sts.
Round 9: Knit.
Round 10: K1, K2tog, K2, K2tog, K2, SSK, K1. 9 sts.
Round 11: K4, K2tog, SSK, K1. 7 sts.

Break yarn, leaving 6" tail. Using the tail, graft the sts closed, grafting the two center sts on the back of the ear into the center st on the front.

With Flamingo, duplicate stitch or embroider a triangle on the front of the ear.

Position the ear on the head between the last two stripes of parchment and roughly between the lines of decreases on the face. Whipstitch or graft the ear to the head with a slight curve. Repeat for second ear.

Embroider face using embroidery floss, and Flamingo for the nose.

Attach tail, using marker at row 65 of Belly for placement on opposite side.

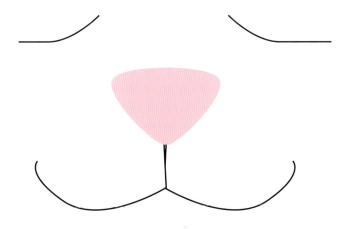

STRIPED PULLOVER

by Kerin Dimeler-Laurence

FINISHED MEASUREMENTS
6 mos (12 mos, 18mos, 2T, 3T, 4T)
21.25 (22, 22.75, 25.25, 26, 26.75)" chest circumference

YARN
Knit Picks Shine Sport (60% Pima Cotton, 40% Modal® natural beech wood fiber; 110 yards/50g):
Orange Version: MC Grapefruit 25778, 2 (2, 2, 3, 3, 3) balls; CC Cream 23615, 1 (2, 2, 2, 2, 3) balls.
Blue Version: MC Reef 25335, 2 (2, 2, 3, 3, 3) balls; CC Cream 23615, 1 (2, 2, 2, 2, 3) balls

NEEDLES
US 3 (3.25 mm) DPNs or 16" circular needles (Magic Loop is not recommended due to stripe technique), or size to obtain gauge

NOTIONS
Yarn Needle
Stitch Markers
Scrap yarn or Stitch Holders
Two 0.5" buttons

GAUGE
24 sts and 33 rows = 4" in St st in the round, blocked.

Striped Pullover

Notes:
Basic stripes decorate this simple pullover. Buttons at the shoulder help with dressing your tots.

Three Needle Bind Off
Hold the two pieces of knitting together with the points of the needles facing to the right. Insert a third needle into the first stitch on each of the needles knitwise, starting with the front needle. Work a knit stitch, pulling the loop through both of the stitches you've inserted the third needle through. After you've pulled the loop through, slip the first stitch off of each of the needles. This takes two stitches (one from the front needle and one from the back) and joins them to make one finished stitch on the third needle (held in your right hand). Repeat this motion, inserting your needle into one stitch on the front and back needles, knitting them together and slipping them off of the needles. Each time you complete a second stitch, pass the first finished stitch over the second and off of the needle (as you would in a traditional bind-off).

K3tog – Knit three stitches together.

P3tog – Purl three stitches together.

K1, p1 Ribbing in the round – Knit in the knit stitches, purl in the purl stitches.

K1, p1 Ribbing flat – RS: K1, p1. WS: P1, k1.

1-row Stripes (worked in the round)
Knit one round in MC, Knit one round in CC.

3-row Stripes
In the round: Knit three rounds in MC, knit three rounds in CC. Carry unused color up the inside of the work.
Worked flat: This is a swing needle technique and must be done with circular or double-pointed needles. Work three rows in St st in MC; do not turn after last row. Slide sts to other side of needle, pick up CC, and work three rows of St st in CC.

DIRECTIONS
Sleeves
Make two identical sleeves. Increases and stripe patterns are worked at the same time; read both sections before proceeding.

With MC, loosely CO 36 (36, 36, 36, 42, 44) sts. PM and join to work in the round, being careful not to twist sts. Work in (K1, P1) rib for 8 rounds.

Increases
Increase Round: K1, M1L, knit to last st, M1R, K1. 2 sts increased.

While maintaining Stripe patterns, work an increase round on the next round, then every 6th (6th, 5th, 6th, 7th, 7th) round 6 (8, 10, 11, 9, 10) times. Work 3 (1, 2, 1, 6, 3) rounds in pattern. 50 (54, 58, 60, 62, 66) sts.

Stripe Patterns
Work in Single-row Stripe pattern for 20 (24, 28, 34, 34, 37) rounds. Work the rest of the sleeve and sleeve cap in Three-row Stripe pattern.

Sleeve Cap
On the next round, BO sts for the sleeve cap: Work in Three-row Stripe pattern to the last 2 sts of the round. BO the last 2 sts of this round and the first two of the next, removing marker. Knit to the end of this row; you will now work flat.

Double Decrease Row: K3tog (RS rows) or P3tog TBL (WS rows) over the first three sts of row; work in pattern to last 3 sts, SSSK or P3tog. 2 sts removed at each edge.

Decrease Row: K2tog (RS rows) or P2tog TBL (WS rows) over the first two sts of row; work in pattern to last 2 sts, SSK or P2tog. 1 st removed at each edge.

Sizes 6 mos (12 mos, 18 mos, 2T): Maintaining Three-Row Stripe pattern, work a Double Decrease Row on the next 1 (1, 2, 2) rows; work a Decrease Row every row 3 (4, 4, 4) times, then every other row 8 (7, 7, 7) times, then every row 3 (4, 4, 6) times; work a Double Decrease Row on the next row. 14 (16, 16, 14) sts.

3T (4T): Maintaining Three-Row Stripe pattern, (work a Double Decrease Row, work a Decrease Row) twice; work a Decrease Row every row 2 (4) times, then every other row 4 times, then on the next third row, then every other row 2 (3) times, then every row 7 (4) times; work a Double Decrease Row on the next row. 14 (18) sts.

All sizes: BO all sts.

Body
With MC, loosely CO 128 (132, 136, 152, 156, 160) sts. PM and join to work in the round, being careful not to twist sts. Work in (K1, P1) rib for 8 rounds.

On the next round, begin Stripe pattern as detailed below, and place a marker after 64 (66, 68, 76, 78, 80) sts to mark the right underarm.

Stripe Pattern
Work in Single Row Stripe pattern for 36 (40, 40, 44, 46, 48) rounds. Work Three-row Stripe pattern for 10 (10, 12, 12, 14, 18) rounds; begin following Armhole directions. Continue in Three-row Stripe for the next 18 (18, 21, 24, 27, 30) rows of the Front and Back; work in MC for the remaining 18 (18, 21, 24, 27, 30) rows.

Armholes
Armhole Decrease Row (RS): K2tog, knit to last 2 sts, SSK. 2 sts decreased.
Armhole Decrease Row (WS): P2tog TBL, purl to last 2 sts, P2tog. 2 sts decreased.

On the next round, stitches are bound off at the underarms and the front and back of the pullover are knit flat separately.

Knit to 3 (2, 2, 4, 3, 3) sts before the right underarm marker. BO the next 6 (4, 4, 8, 6, 6) sts, removing marker. Knit to 3 (2, 2, 4, 3, 3) sts before the end of the round; BO the last 3 (2, 2, 4, 3, 3) sts of this round and the first 3 (2, 2, 4, 3, 3) sts of the next. Continue knitting across Front. Place 58 (62, 64, 68, 72, 74) Back sts on scrap yarn or a stitch holder and work Front.

Maintaining Stripe pattern, work an Armhole decrease on the next row, then:

6 mos: On the next second row, then on the next fourth row, then on the next fifth row. Work 5 rows plain. 50 sts.

12 mos: On the next third row, then on the next fifth row. Work 10 rows plain. 56 sts.

18 mos: On the next second row, then on the next fourth row, then on the next fifth row. Work 10 rows plain. 56 sts.

2T: On the next second row, then on the next third row, then on the next sixth row. Work 11 rows plain. 60 sts.

3T: On the next row, then on the next second row, then every fourth row twice. Work 15 rows plain. 62 sts.

4T: On the next row, then on the next second row, then every fourth row twice; work 8 rows plain, work an Armhole Decrease Row. Work 8 rows plain. 62 sts.

Neckline
On the next row, stitches are bound off at the front neck to begin the neckline; work the right and left shoulders together to the end using separate balls of yarn. At this point you should only be using MC.

RS: K 22 (25, 25, 26, 26, 27), BO the next 6 (6, 6, 8, 10, 8) sts, work across remaining 22 (25, 25, 26, 26, 27) sts. On the next row, purl to 3 sts before neckline edge, P3tog, attach a second ball at right neckline edge, SSSP, P to end. Continue working both shoulders at once.

Sizes 6 mos: On the next row, K3tog at right neckline edge, and SSSK at left neckline edge. 4 sts decreased.

Neckline Decrease Row:
RS Rows: K to last 2 sts of left neck edge, SSK. K2tog, K across right shoulder.
WS Rows: P to last 2 sts of right neck edge, P2tog. P2tog TBL, P across left shoulder.
1 st removed at Neckline edge.

All Sizes: Work a Neckline Decrease Row every row 1 (4, 6, 6, 4, 4) times, then every other row 4 (4, 2, 1, 3, 2) times, then every third row 0 (0, 0, 1, 1, 1) time. Work 1 (1, 3, 3, 3, 5) rows in St st. Place remaining 13 (15, 15, 16, 16, 18) sts of each shoulder on scrap yarn or a spare needles.

Back
Place 58 (62, 64, 68, 72, 74) Back sts on the needles. Attach yarn ready to begin a RS row. Maintaining Stripe pattern, work Armhole decreases as worked on the Front. Work in Stockinette st, following Stripe Sequence as given, and switching to MC when directed.

One row before the last row given for the MC section, work across 14 (16, 16, 17, 17, 19) sts, BO the next 22 (24, 24, 26, 28, 24) sts, then work across the remaining 14 (16, 16, 17, 17, 19) sts. On the next row, K 12 (14, 14, 15, 15, 17), K2tog across first shoulder; attach yarn at the neckline edge of the other shoulder and SSK, K to end. 13 (15, 15, 16, 16, 18) sts.

Work the right (as worn) shoulder in Garter st (knit every row) for 10 rows to make a stable band. BO all sts on right shoulder. Leave Left shoulder sts on a spare needle.

Finishing
Turn sweater inside out. Holding both sides of the left shoulder together, work a three needle BO across all sts.

Collar
Turn sweater right side out. With MC and starting at the front right shoulder, PU and K 32 (32, 36, 40, 44, 46) sts across the front neckline to the left shoulder, then PU and K 26 (28, 28, 30, 32, 32) across the Back neckline to the right shoulder. PU and K 6 sts across the garter st band. 64 (66, 70, 76, 82, 84) sts on the needles.

Work in (K1, P1) rib for 8 rows. BO all sts loosely in pattern.

Buttonhole band
With RS facing, place 13 (15, 15, 16, 16, 18) sts of the Right front shoulder on the needles, and attach yarn ready to begin a RS row. Work across these sts in (K1, P1) rib, Then PU and work 6 sts in rib as established across the edge of the collar. 19 (21, 21, 22, 22, 24) sts on the needles.

Work two rows in Rib.

On the next row, work buttonholes: Work 4 sts in rib, K2tog, YO twice, SSK, work in rib for 5 sts, K2tog, YO twice, SSK, work in rib to end.

On the next row, work in rib, working one knit and one purl st into each double YO to match established rib pattern. Work in rib for three more rows, then BO all sts loosely in pattern.

Hold the two sides of the right shoulder together, with the last rows of St st from each side overlapping (ribbed band on top). At armhole edge, whipstitch the two layers together along the garter st band. This will line up the shoulders for setting in the sleeves.

Set in Sleeves
With right sides facing out, set sleeves into armhole openings, making sure that the center of each sleeve cap is placed at the shoulder seam and that the seam under the sleeve and bound off sts of the armhole are centered. Pin in place. Using yarn needle and yarn, begin at the underarm and sew sleeves into the armholes, using mattress stitch.

Sew buttons to shoulder under the buttonholes. Weave in ends, wash and block.

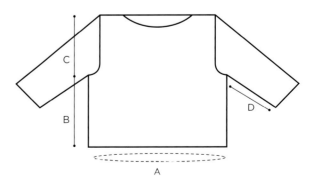

A 21.3 (22, 22.7, 25.3, 26, 26.7)"
B 6.5 (7, 7.25, 7.75, 8.25, 9)"
C 4.7 (5.1, 5.4, 5.6, 5.6, 6)"
D 5.8 (7, 7.3, 9.1, 9.3, 9.8)"

Knit Picks yarn is both luxe and affordable—a seeming contradiction trounced! But it's not just about the pretty colors; we also care deeply about fiber quality and fair labor practices, leaving you with a gorgeously reliable product you'll turn to time and time again.

This collection features

Shine Sport
Sport Weight
60% Pima Cotton, 40% Modal

Comfy Sport
Sport Weight
75% Pima Cotton, 25% Acrylic

Swish DK
DK Weight
100% Superwash Merino Wool

Comfy Worsted
Worsted Weight
75% Pima Cotton, 25% Acrylic

Stroll Sock
Fingering Weight
75% Superwash Merino Wool, 25% Nylon

View these beautiful yarns and more at www.KnitPicks.com

Abbreviations							
BO	bind off	M	marker	Rev St st	reverse stockinette stitch	St st	stockinette stitch
cn	cable needle	M1	make one stitch			sts	stitch(es)
CC	contrast color	M1L	make one left-leaning stitch	RH	right hand	TBL	through back loop
CO	cast on			rnd(s)	round(s)	TFL	through front loop
cont	continue	M1R	make one right-leaning stitch	RS	right side	tog	together
dec	decrease(es)			Sk	skip	W&T	wrap & turn (see specific instructions in pattern)
DPN(s)	double pointed needle(s)	MC	main color	Sk2p	sl 1, k2tog, pass slipped stitch over k2tog: 2 sts dec		
		P	purl			WE	work even
EOR	every other row	P2tog	purl 2 sts together			WS	wrong side
inc	increase	PM	place marker	SKP	sl, k, psso: 1 st dec	WYIB	with yarn in back
K	knit	PFB	purl into the front and back of stitch	SL	slip	WYIF	with yarn in front
K2tog	knit two sts together			SM	slip marker	YO	yarn over
KFB	knit into the front and back of stitch	PSSO	pass slipped stitch over	SSK	sl, sl, k these 2 sts tog		
				SSsP	sl, sl, sl, p these 2 sts tog tbl		
K-wise	knitwise	PU	pick up				
		P-wise	purlwise	SSSK	sl, sl, sl, k these 3 sts tog		
LH	left hand	rep	repeat				